LEARNING ABOUT
Plants

Catherine Veitch

Raintree

Chicago, Illinois

T0050871

The author would like to dedicate this book to her mother,
Jacqueline Veitch, who inspired her with a love of nature.

Edited by Dan Nunn, Rebecca Rissman,
and Sian Smith
Designed by Joanna Hinton-Malivoire
Picture research by Mica Brancic
Production by Sophia Argyris
Originated by Capstone Global Library Ltd
Printed in the United States of America in
North Mankato, MN. 012014 007974RP

Library of Congress Cataloging-in-Publication Data
Veitch, Catherine.
  Learning about plants / Catherine Veitch.—1st ed.
      p. cm.—(The natural world)
  Includes bibliographical references and index.
ISBN 978-1-4109-5401-5 (hb)
ISBN 978-1-4109-5406-0 (pb)
1. Plants—Juvenile literature. I. Title. II. Series: Natural
world (Chicago, Ill.)

  QK49.V38 2013
  580—dc23   2012049392

Acknowledgments
The author and publisher are grateful to the
following for permission to reproduce copyright
material: Alamy: Imagebroker.net, 4 (top inset),
24; Science Source: Dr Jeremy Burgess, 4 (bottom
inset), 23; Shutterstock: a9photo, back cover, 20,
Anest, 16 (inset), Antonio Abrignani, 12 (inset), 23,
aodaodaodaod, 13, Chepko Danil Vitalevich,
24 (top), Dave Head, 5, 24, de2marco, 10 (inset),
22, ER_09, 16, Gabriela Insuratelu, 18, Galyna
Andrushko, 6, Igor Normann, 4, 22, Katharina
Wittfeld, 19, 24, LianeM, cover, Martin Fowler, 12,
23, Maxim Blinkov, 11, Neirfy, 8, 22, Panitchon, 7,
saiva_l, 17, Serg64, 14, 22, Sergey Galushko, 15, 23,
szabozoltan, 9, 23, Timolina, 10, yuriy kulik, 21.

We would like to thank Michael Bright for his
invaluable help in the preparation of this book.

Every effort has been made to contact copyright
holders of any material reproduced in this book.
Any omissions will be rectified in subsequent
printings if notice is given to the publisher.

Contents

Blackberry

thorn

fruit

roots

4

Bluebell

petal

stem

5

Bulrush

flower

stem

Cosmos

petal

stem

7

Freesia

bud

flower

seed pod

seed

Hyacinth

flower

bulb

Ivy

leaf

stem

Orchid

pollen

petal

12

Pitcher Plant

leaf

Poppy

bud

stem

Rose

bud

leaf

thorn

15

Strawberry

seed

fruit

petal

stem

17

Teasel

stem

flower head

Tomato

fruit

vine

19

leaf

Water Lily

flower

leaf

21

Picture Glossary

 **bud** part of a plant that grows into a new leaf or a flower

 **bulb** some plants grow out of bulbs in the ground. Bulbs are like food stores. Food in the bulb helps a plant grow.

 **flower** part of a plant that makes seeds. The smells flowers make and their colors help attract insects.

 **fruit** fruits hold seeds. Plants make fruit so that animals will eat the fruit and carry the seeds to new places.

 **leaf** part of a plant. Leaves use sunlight to make food for the plant.

 **petal** one of the colored parts of a flower

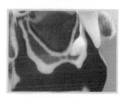 **pollen** powder inside a flower. Pollen has to move from flower to flower or plant to plant for plants to make seeds.

 **roots** part of a plant that holds the plant in the ground. Roots bring water to the plant.

 **seed pod** case that holds seeds and helps keep them safe

seeds plants make seeds. Seeds grow into new plants.

stem part of a plant from which the leaves and flowers grow. Stems hold plants up and carry water to different parts of the plant.

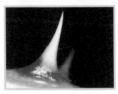

thorn hard, sharp point that sticks out from the stems of some plants. Thorns help stop animals from eating the plant.

vine long, winding stem that creeps along the ground or climbs up things

Notes for Parents and Teachers

- Go on a nature walk with the children. Help them identify different plants and their parts. Children can sketch or photograph what they see.
  Use the pictures to create a class book.
- Collect different flowers and leaves. Discuss the different shapes and colors of the flowers and leaves. Press the flowers and add these and the leaves to the class book.
  Remind children to always check with an adult that flowers and leaves are safe to collect, and to always wash their hands after handling flowers and leaves.